Earth, Moon, and Sun System

Contents

Build Reading Skills
Preview the Book

You read nonfiction books like this one to learn about new ideas. Be sure to look through, or *preview*, the book before you start to read.

First, look at the title, front cover, and table of contents. What do you guess you will read about? Think about what you already know about Earth, the Moon, and the Sun.

Next, look through the book page by page. Read the headings and the words in bold type. Look at the pictures and captions. Notice that each new part of the book starts with a big photograph. What other special features do you find in the book?

Headings, captions, and other features of nonfiction books are like road signs. They can help you find your way through new information. Now you are ready to read!

What Are Earth, the Moon, and the Sun?

MAKE A CONNECTION
The Moon is an object that is close to Earth in space. The Sun is much farther away. What do you know about the Moon and the Sun?

FIND OUT ABOUT
- Earth, the Moon, and the Sun
- Earth's place in the solar system

VOCABULARY

Earth

Earth is our home planet. A **planet** is a large, nearly round object that moves around a star. A **star** is a huge ball of very hot, glowing gases. The **Sun** is a star. Earth moves in a path around, or **revolves** around, the Sun. Earth also spins somewhat like a top, or **rotates**, as it moves through space.

Earth's surface is hard and rocky. It has tall mountains, flat plains, and deep valleys. Close to three-fourths of Earth is covered by water.

Earth has a layer of gases around it called an atmosphere. Earth's atmosphere is made mostly of nitrogen gas. It also has oxygen, carbon dioxide, and other gases.

▲ Earth is home to many living things. Earth is one of eight planets that revolve around the Sun.

Earth is the only planet known to support life. Earth's atmosphere has gases, such as oxygen, that living things need. Earth's atmosphere and distance from the Sun help Earth stay at temperatures that support life. Earth also has water in liquid form. Living things need water.

 What does Earth have that living things need?

EARTH

FACTS

- **Diameter:**
  12,756 km (about 7,926 mi)

- **Surface:**
  rocky with oceans, plains, mountains, volcanoes, and some craters

- **Surface Temperature:**
  -88°C to 58°C (about -126°F to 136°F)

- **Moons:** 1

- **Average Distance From Sun:**
  about 150 million km (about 93 million mi)

FURTHER FACTS

- Earth moves quickly through space at an average speed of 107,229 km (about 66,629 mi) per hour.

- Earth is sometimes called the blue planet.

▲ Sometimes we see the Moon at night. Sometimes we see it in the daytime.

▲ The surface of the Moon has many large craters.

Earth's Moon

A **moon** is a natural, rocky or icy object that revolves around a planet. Earth has one moon. The Moon does not make its own light. We see the Moon because light from the Sun bounces, or reflects, off the Moon.

The Moon revolves around Earth. The Moon also rotates. The Moon takes the same amount of time to rotate once as to revolve once. So the same side of the Moon always faces Earth.

The Moon is different from Earth in many ways. The Moon has no liquid water and almost no atmosphere. And the Moon gets much hotter and much colder than Earth. The Moon also has many more craters. A **crater** is a bowl-shaped landform.

Twelve astronauts walked on the Moon between 1969 and 1972. ▶

Scientists have explored the Moon using spacecraft. A spacecraft called Luna 3 flew by the Moon in 1959. It took the first pictures of the side of the Moon that faces away from Earth. Astronauts first landed on the Moon in 1969 during the Apollo 11 mission. They collected rocks for scientists to study. After that, astronauts took other trips to the Moon to keep exploring.

 How is the Moon different from Earth?

EARTH'S MOON

FACTS

- **Diameter:**
  3,475 km (about 2,160 mi), about one-fourth the diameter of Earth

- **Surface:**
  rocky with craters, cliffs, and plains

- **Surface Temperature:**
  -233°C to 123°C (about -387°F to 253°F)

- **Atmosphere:** almost none

- **Average Distance From Earth:**
  384,400 km (about 238,855 mi)

FURTHER FACTS

- Many craters on the Moon were made by meteorites. A *meteorite* is a small chunk of rock or metal from space that hits a planet or a moon.

The Sun

The Sun is the closest star to Earth. So it looks much bigger to us than other stars do. The Sun is a medium-sized star of average brightness. But the Sun is huge compared to Earth. More than a million Earths could fit inside the Sun!

The Sun is made mostly of the gases hydrogen and helium. Inside the Sun, hydrogen is changed into helium. This gives off huge amounts of energy. It is not safe to look right at the Sun.

Earth gets heat and light energy from the Sun. Most living things depend on the Sun's energy. It helps keep Earth at temperatures that support life. Also, plants use light energy from the Sun, along with air and water,

The Sun is the main source of energy for living things on Earth. ▼

to make their own food. Energy in that food passes to animals that eat plants.

Energy from the Sun also powers Earth's winds, ocean currents, and the water cycle. The water cycle is the movement of water from Earth's surface to the atmosphere and back again. Clouds and rain are parts of the water cycle.

People have found ways to use energy from the Sun, or solar energy. Solar panels on buildings change solar energy into electricity.

 What kind of space object is the Sun? What is the Sun made of?

SUN

FACTS

- **Diameter:**
  1,390,000 km (about 864,000 mi)

- **Surface:**
  hot, glowing gases

- **Surface Temperature:**
  about 5,500°C (about 10,000°F)

- **Core, or Center, Temperature:**
  over 15 million °C (about 27 million °F)

FURTHER FACTS

- The Sun has an atmosphere.

- Solar flares are strong bursts of energy given off by the Sun.

- Sunspots are cooler places on the Sun's surface.

- Prominences are huge loops of glowing gas that stretch out from the Sun.

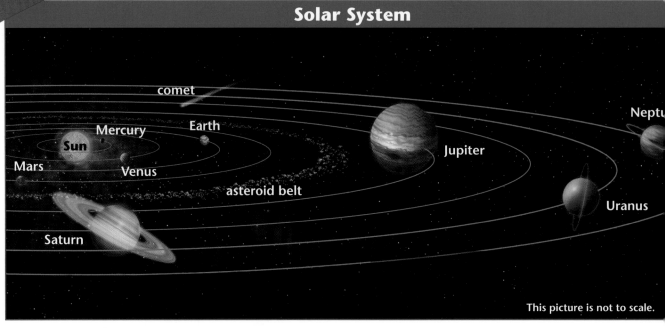

This picture is not to scale.

▲ Our solar system includes the Sun and the objects that revolve around it.

The Solar System

A **solar system** is a star and all the objects that revolve around that star. The Sun is at the center of our solar system. It is the largest object in it. Eight planets revolve around the Sun. Earth is the third planet from the Sun.

Our solar system also has many smaller objects. For example, many planets have moons. Comets and asteroids are other objects. They revolve around the Sun. Comets are made of frozen gases, ice, rock, and dust. Asteroids are made of rock, metal, or both. Most asteroids are in the asteroid belt. It is an area between Mars and Jupiter.

An **orbit** is the path an object takes as it revolves around another object. The farther a planet is from the Sun, the larger the planet's orbit.

The planet Venus can sometimes be seen in the night sky. It is shown here just above the Moon. ▶

Mercury, Venus, Earth, and Mars are the *inner planets.* They are closest to the Sun. These planets are small and dense. Their surfaces are solid and rocky. The inner planets have few or no moons.

Jupiter, Saturn, Uranus, and Neptune are the *outer planets.* These planets are very far from the Sun, so they are very cold. The outer planets are huge. They have rings and many moons. These planets are made mostly of gas. They are often called the gas giants.

Objects in our solar system stay in their orbits because of gravity. Gravity is the force that pulls all objects toward one another.

 Tell about some kinds of objects in the solar system.

REFLECT ON READING

You previewed pictures, captions, and other book features before reading. Tell how one picture helped you better understand Earth, the Moon, or the Sun.

APPLY SCIENCE CONCEPTS

Imagine exploring the surface of the Moon. Write in your science notebook about special clothing, vehicles, or equipment you think you might need. Why would you need it?

Sequence

Sequence is the order in which events or steps happen. Sequence is sometimes called time order or chronological order.

As you read page 19, notice what steps take place in the lunar cycle.

TIPS

Thinking about the sequence of events can help you understand what you read.

- Ask yourself, "What happens first?" "What happens next?" and "What happens last?"
- Words such as *first, next, then, after, last,* and *finally* can be clues to the order of events or steps.
- Think about why the order of events is important.

A sequence chart can help you keep track of a sequence of events.

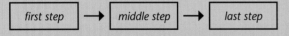

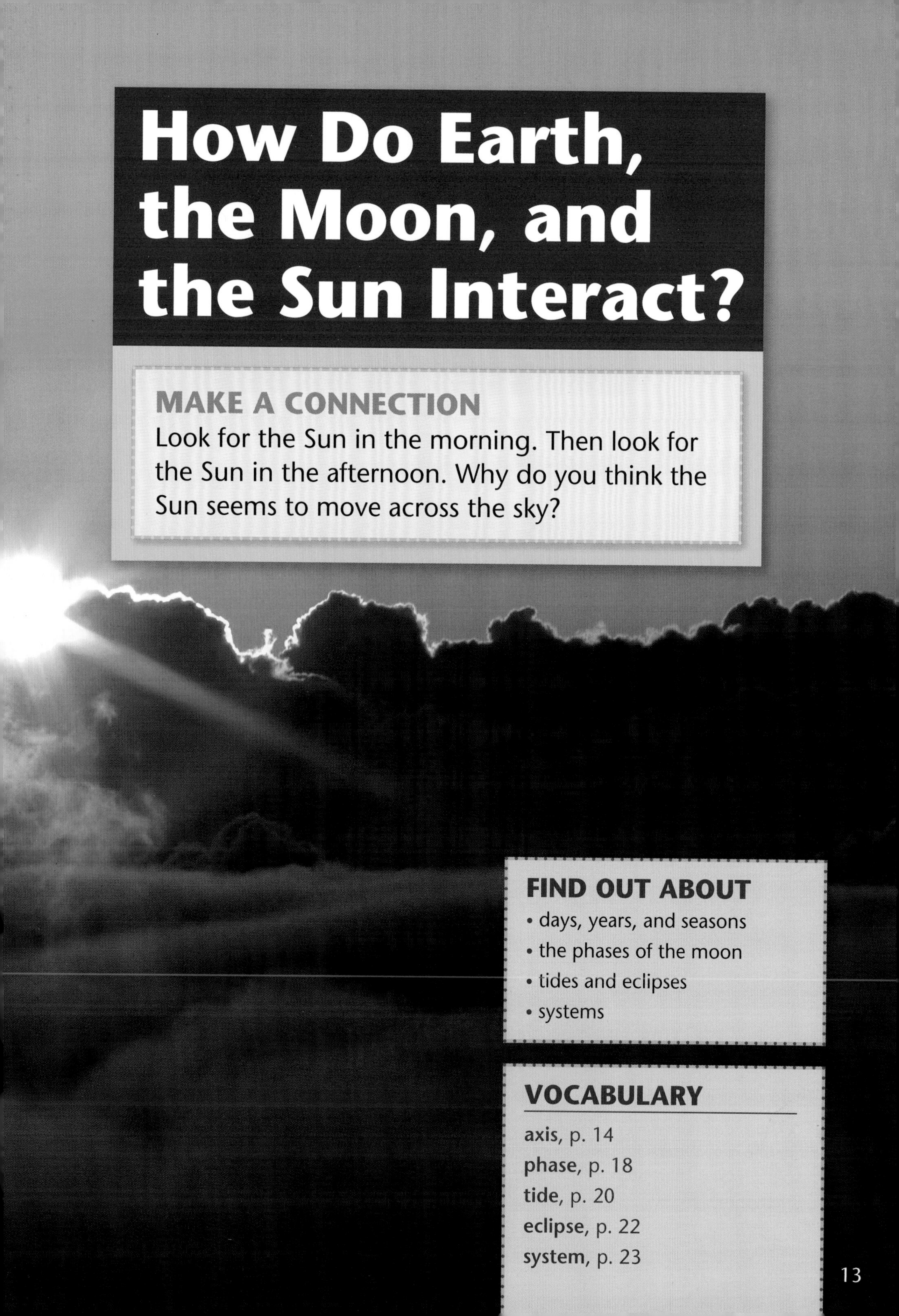

How Do Earth, the Moon, and the Sun Interact?

MAKE A CONNECTION

Look for the Sun in the morning. Then look for the Sun in the afternoon. Why do you think the Sun seems to move across the sky?

FIND OUT ABOUT

- days, years, and seasons
- the phases of the moon
- tides and eclipses
- systems

VOCABULARY

axis, p. 14
phase, p. 18
tide, p. 20
eclipse, p. 22
system, p. 23

Day and Night

axis

Earth

Sun

This picture is not to scale.

Day and night happen because Earth rotates on its axis. ▶

Earth and the Sun

Days

Earth rotates around an imaginary center line. This line is called Earth's **axis**.

A day is the amount of time a planet takes to rotate once. Earth's day is about 24 hours long. As a planet rotates, the part of the planet that faces the Sun has daylight. The part that is turned away from the Sun has darkness, or night.

On Earth, we can see changes caused by Earth's rotation. The Sun, Moon, and stars seem to rise in the east. Then they seem to move slowly across the sky and set in the west. Shadows change in length and position as the Sun's position in the sky changes.

When the Sun is high in the sky, shadows are shorter. When the Sun is lower, shadows are longer. ▶

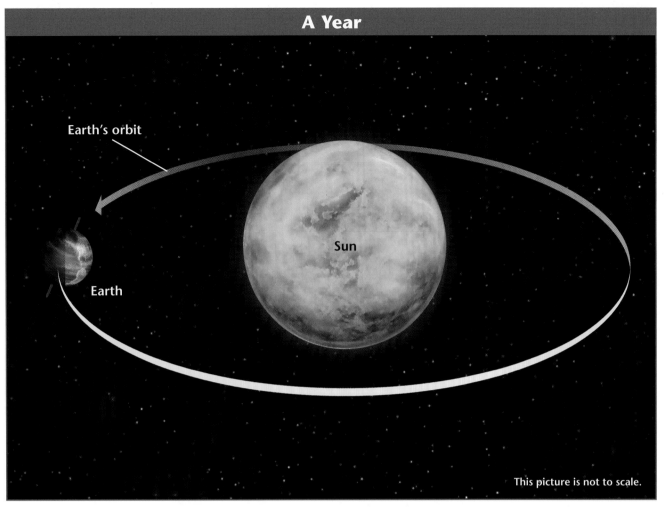

Earth's orbit

Earth

Sun

This picture is not to scale.

▲ Earth moves in an orbit around the Sun. A year is the time
a planet takes to revolve once around the Sun.

Years

A year is the amount of time a planet takes to revolve
once around the Sun. Earth's year is about 365 days long.
Other planets take different amounts of time to revolve
once around the Sun.

Earth's orbit around the Sun is not a perfect circle. It is
more like an oval, or ellipse. Because of this, Earth is a little
closer to the Sun in January than it is in July.

Seasons

Earth has four seasons because its axis is tilted. As Earth revolves around the Sun, this tilt causes parts of Earth to point more toward the Sun. Other parts of Earth point more away from the Sun.

The equator is an imaginary line that divides Earth into two halves. The halves are called the Northern Hemisphere and the Southern Hemisphere. When the Northern Hemisphere is tilted *toward* the Sun, the Sun's rays hit it more directly. This part of Earth has summer. The Sun appears higher in the sky. There are more hours of daylight. Temperatures are warmer.

When the Northern Hemisphere is tilted *away* from the Sun, the Sun's rays hit it less directly. Now this part of Earth has winter. The Sun appears lower in the sky. There are fewer hours of daylight. Temperatures are colder.

The tilt of Earth's axis causes the seasons. ▶

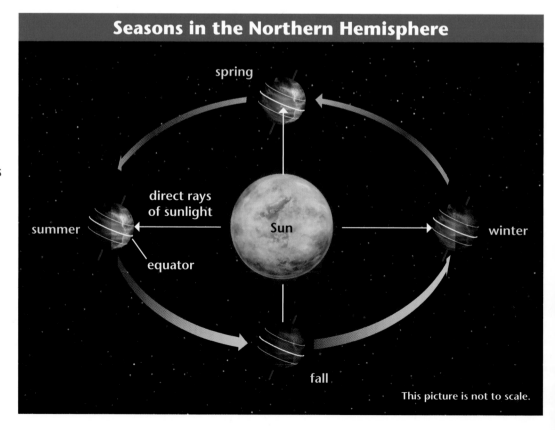

Seasons in the Northern Hemisphere

spring

direct rays of sunlight

summer

Sun

winter

equator

fall

This picture is not to scale.

winter

In the winter, we have fewer hours of daylight. Temperatures are colder. ▶

The number of hours of daylight changes little by little during the year. One day each year has the most hours of daylight. That day is called the summer solstice. In the Northern Hemisphere, the summer solstice happens on June 20 or 21. It is the start of summer.

One day each year has the fewest hours of daylight. That day is called the winter solstice. In the Northern Hemisphere, the winter solstice happens on December 21 or 22. It is the start of winter.

 Why does Earth have seasons?

◀ The way the Moon looks from Earth changes. The different shapes we see are called phases.

Earth, the Moon, and the Sun

Phases of the Moon

Remember that the Moon does not give off light. Like Earth, the Moon is lighted by the Sun. And like Earth, the Moon rotates. As the Moon rotates, different parts face the Sun. At any time, the side of the Moon facing the Sun is lighted. The side of the Moon turned away from the Sun is dark.

The Moon's shape seems to change during the month. We call the different shapes that we see **phases**.

The Moon does not actually change shape. The phases of the Moon happen because the Moon revolves around Earth. As the Moon moves in its orbit, we see more or less of the side of the Moon that is lighted by the Sun.

The Moon has eight phases. ▼

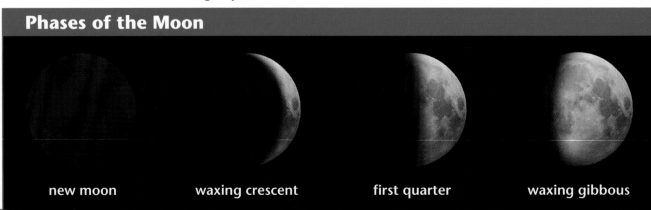

Phases of the Moon

| new moon | waxing crescent | first quarter | waxing gibbous |

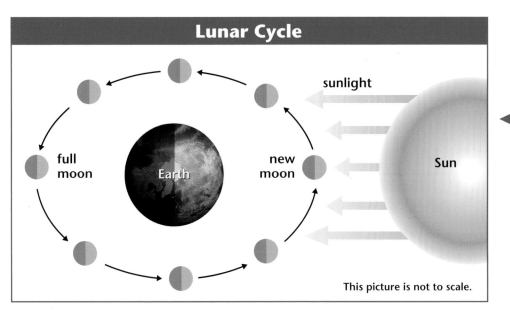

Lunar Cycle

sunlight

full moon

Earth

new moon

Sun

This picture is not to scale.

The lunar cycle takes about $29\frac{1}{2}$ days. A month is a unit of time based on the lunar cycle.

The phases of the Moon change in a repeating pattern. This pattern is called the lunar cycle.

First, we have the new moon phase. The side of the Moon that is lighted faces away from Earth. So we do not see the Moon.

The Moon moves in its orbit. Each night we see more and more of the Moon's lighted side. We say the Moon is *waxing*. After two weeks, we see the whole side of the Moon that is lighted. This is the full moon phase.

Then, in the two weeks after a full moon, we see less and less of the Moon's lighted side. We say the Moon is *waning*. Finally, the cycle begins again with the new moon phase.

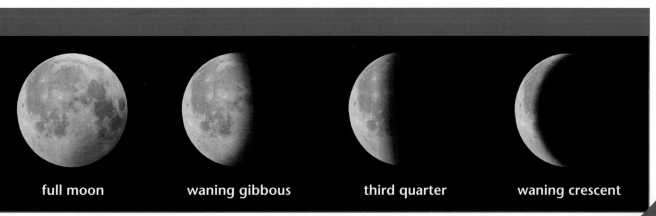

full moon   waning gibbous   third quarter   waning crescent

Tides

At the seashore, you can see that the water level in the ocean is always changing. The regular rise and fall of the water level is called the **tide**. The tide is caused mainly by gravity between Earth and the Moon, together with Earth's movement in space.

Earth and the Moon pull on each other. The Moon's pull on Earth is strongest on the side of Earth closest to the Moon. A bulge of ocean water forms on that part of Earth. The bulge is a *high tide*. The water level is the highest at high tide. The opposite side of Earth also has a high tide, mostly because of Earth's movement. Other places on Earth have a low water level, or *low tide*.

These pictures show high tide (left) and low tide (right) at the Bay of Fundy in Nova Scotia, Canada.

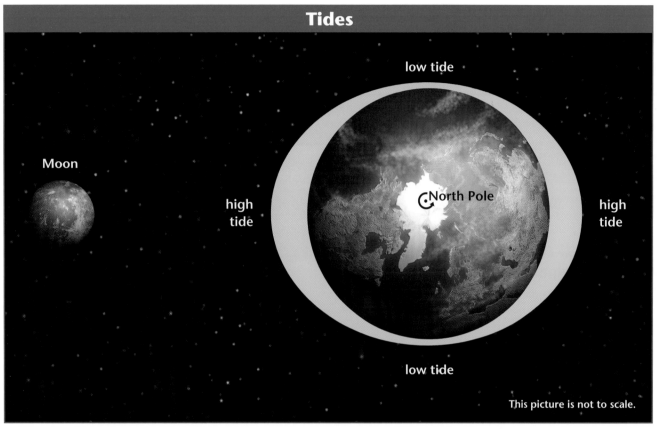

Tides

Moon

low tide

high tide

North Pole

high tide

low tide

This picture is not to scale.

▲ Tides are caused mainly by gravity between Earth and the Moon, together with Earth's movement in space.

As Earth rotates, different places on Earth have high tide and low tide. Most shorelines have two high tides and two low tides about every 24 hours.

Gravity between Earth and the Sun also affects tides. The effects of the Sun are not as great as those of the Moon. This is because the Sun is much farther away. But the Sun can make the Moon's effects stronger or weaker. For example, sometimes the Moon, Earth, and the Sun are in a straight line. High tides are higher and low tides are lower when this happens.

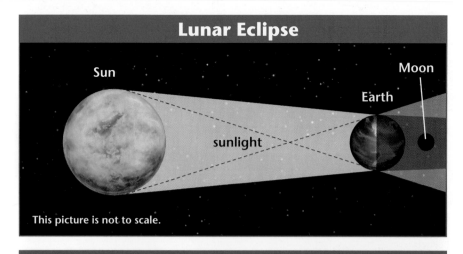

During a lunar eclipse, the Moon passes through Earth's shadow. ▶

During a solar eclipse, Earth passes through the Moon's shadow. ▶

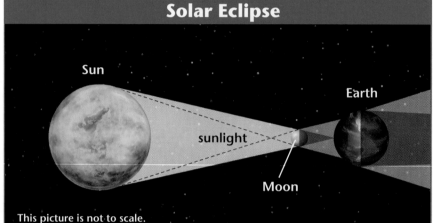

Eclipses

Objects make shadows when they block light from reaching other objects. Sometimes a moon or a planet moves into the shadow of another space object. This is called an **eclipse**.

A *lunar eclipse* happens when the Moon passes through Earth's shadow. Remember that the Moon is lighted by the Sun. When the Moon moves into Earth's shadow, Earth blocks sunlight from reaching the Moon. The Moon becomes dark for a while. You can watch a lunar eclipse safely without eye protection.

A *solar eclipse* happens when Earth passes through the Moon's shadow. In some places on Earth, the view of the Sun is blocked by the Moon. Never watch a solar eclipse by looking right at the Sun. This could seriously hurt your eyes.

 The Moon seems to change shape during the month. Why do the phases of the Moon happen?

Together, Earth, the Moon, and the Sun are a system.

This picture is not to scale.

About Systems

A **system** is a group of related parts that form a whole. The parts affect one another, or interact.

You learned about our solar system. The Sun, the planets, and many other objects are parts of this system. They interact because of gravity.

We can think of Earth and the Sun as a system with two parts. Interactions in this system cause day and night. They also cause seasons.

Earth, the Moon, and the Sun form a system with three parts. Interactions in this system cause the phases of the Moon. They also cause tides and eclipses.

 What is a system? Give an example.

REFLECT ON READING

Work with a group to make eight cards. On each card, draw a moon phase. Write its name. Take turns putting the cards in order, or sequence. Start with the new moon.

APPLY SCIENCE CONCEPTS

Find out about future lunar or solar eclipses that can be seen from your area. Use books or the Internet. As a class, make a list. Include the date and kind of each eclipse.

Glossary

axis (AK-sis) an imaginary line that goes through the center of an object, around which the object spins, or rotates **(14)**

crater (KRAY-tuhr) a bowl-shaped landform made when a meteorite or other space object hits the surface of a planet or a moon **(6)**

eclipse (ih-KLIPS) when one object in space moves into the shadow made by another object **(22)**

moon (MOON) a natural, rocky or icy object that revolves around a planet **(6)**

orbit (OR-bit) the path an object takes as it revolves around another object in space **(10)**

phase (FAYZ) any of the different shapes the Moon appears to have when seen from Earth **(18)**

planet (PLAN-it) a large, nearly round object that revolves around a star **(4)**

revolve (rih-VAHLV) to move in a path, or orbit, around another object **(4)**

rotate (RO-tayt) to spin on an axis **(4)**

solar system (SOH-luhr SIS-tuhm) a star and the planets, their moons, and other objects that revolve around that star **(10)**

star (STAHR) a huge ball of very hot, glowing gases in space that gives off energy **(4)**

Sun (SUHN) the star that is at the center of our solar system **(4)**

system (SIS-tuhm) a group of related parts that form a whole **(23)**

tide (TYDE) the regular rise and fall of the water level of Earth's oceans **(20)**